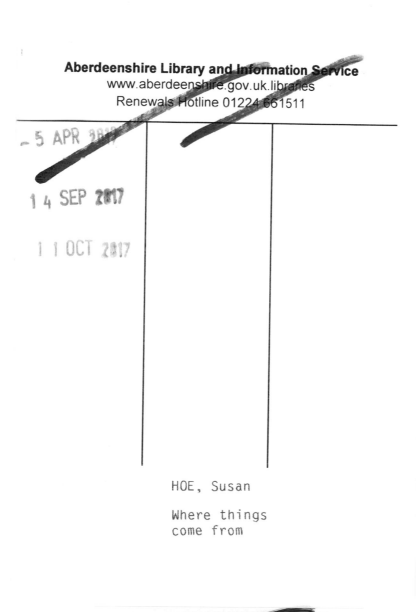

USING MAPS

Where things come from

by Susan Hoe

ticktock

By Susan Hoe
Series consultant: Debra Voege
Editor: Mark Sachner
Project manager: Joe Harris
ticktock designer: Hayley Terry
Picture research: Lizzie Knowles and Joe Harris
We would like to thank Phil Mayes and the staff of Bean Chocolate
(www.beanchocolate.com).

Copyright © 2008 ticktock Entertainment Ltd.
First published in Great Britain by ticktock Media Ltd.,
Unit 2, Orchard Business Centre, North Farm Road, Tunbridge Wells, Kent TN2 3XF, Great Britain.

A CIP catalogue record for this book is available from the British Library.

ISBN 978 1 84696 724 5

Printed in China

PICTURE CREDITS

Peter Bull Art Studio: 14, 31b. Dean Conger/ Corbis: 20br. Getmapping PLC: 24tc. Image100/ SuperStock: 7b. iStock: 17tl, 19t, 19br, 21b, 22t, 25b, 27 (oil barrel). Jupiter Images: 2, 6t, 13tr. www.mapart.co.uk: 7t, 12, 13b, 17b, 18, 22b, 23, 26, 30. Iain Masterton/ Alamy: 17tr. MIXA. Co., Ltd./ Alamy: 4t. Ulli Seer/ Getty Images: 5t. Shutterstock: 6b, 10all, 13tl, 15 all, 19tr, 19bl, 24tl, 24b, 25t, 25c, 27 all (except oil barrel). Justin Spain: 4c, 9 all, 21t, 31t. Hayley Terry: 5b, 11. Tim Thirlaway: 28, 29. ticktock Media archive: 4b, 8. Steve Vidler/ SuperStock: 17cr, 20bl.

Contents

What is a map? 4

Why do we need maps? 6

Mapping a sweet shop 8

Mapping a shopping centre 10

A map of our country's resources 12

Mapping our world 14

A world trade map 16

Mapping goods from China 18

Mapping a tea farm in China 20

Drawing maps 22

Hi-tech mapmaking 24

Choosing goods to import 26

Making your own shopping centre map 28

Glossary 30

Index 32

Words in **bold** are explained in the glossary.

What is a map?

A map is a drawing of a certain place. The place is usually shown from above.

This place can be as big as the whole world. Or it can be as small as your local sweet shop!

Making a map of an island

Map Key

Trees/woods

Roads/footpaths

Grey-roofed building

Red-roofed building

Pier

Gardens

Maps help us find things us if we were directly above them.

In this book, we are going to see how maps show us about where things come from. But first let's look at some of the ways that maps can help us.

Find a group of trees in the photograph.

Now find them on the map.

Why do we need maps?

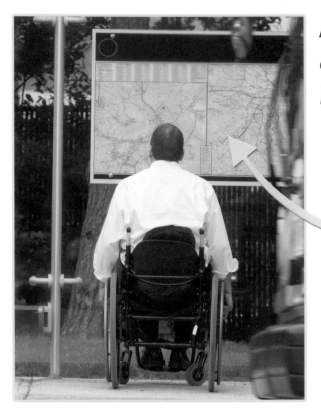

Maps help us find our way around. They give us all kinds of information about where we live!

A map can help you get from one place to another. It can show you where you are, where you want to go, and how to get there.

Weather map of the UK and Ireland

This map shows you what the weather will be like where you live.

Can you tell what kinds of weather this map is showing?

World map

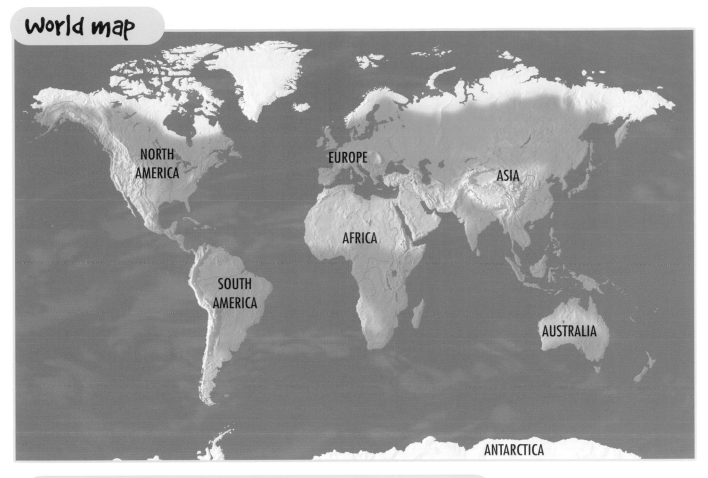

NORTH AMERICA

EUROPE

ASIA

AFRICA

SOUTH AMERICA

AUSTRALIA

ANTARCTICA

This map shows the world's deserts in yellow. The forests and woods are in green. Places covered in snow and ice are white.

Maps teach us important facts about places. These places might be close to home or far away. Maps show us whether the land is flat or hilly.

They can show what crops are grown and what kinds of things are made in certain places. Maps can show what kinds of animals live in different places.

Maps are handy and easy to use. They can show us huge areas in a small amount of space. We can take them just about anywhere!

Mapping a sweet shop

Maps show how a place looks if you are looking down on it. That place can be a country, a town, or even your favourite sweet shop!

A 3-D sweet shop

This sweet shop is a solid, or **three-dimensional** (**3-D**), space. The shop and the things in the shop are solid. They have length, width, and **depth**.

A 2-D map

A map is a flat, or **two-dimensional (2-D)**, drawing of a space. In a map, all of the objects in the shop look flat. They have length and width only. Let's see how we can make a solid room look flat.

To create the 2-D map, we draw all the flat shapes on a piece of paper.

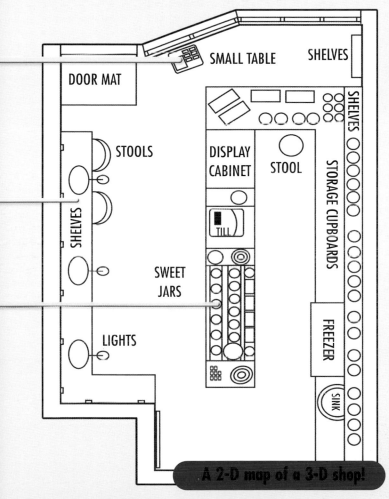

A 2-D map of a 3-D shop!

DOOR MAT

SMALL TABLE

SHELVES

STOOLS

SHELVES

DISPLAY CABINET

STOOL

STORAGE CUPBOARDS

SHELVES

TILL

SWEET JARS

FREEZER

LIGHTS

SINK

This map shows you how to find everything in the shop.

Find the stools.

Find the sweet jars.

This 3-D drawing of the shop was made from the photograph.

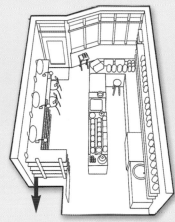

Pretend you are able to float up above the sweet shop and look down on it.

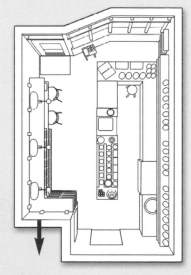

To create the 2-D map, draw all of the sweet shop shapes that you see from above on a piece of paper. Make them flat shapes.

Mapping a shopping centre

We have just made a map of a sweet shop. But you can also use maps to show larger areas. When you look at a map of a shopping centre, you can see all the shops. The map tells you where to find each one.

A 3-D walkway in a shopping centre.

This photo shows many shops in a shopping centre. They are in the photo, but they may be hard to find without a map.

Shopping – a window to the world!

When you're in a shopping centre, you can buy things from all over the world! People who buy these **products** are called consumers.

Tea from China

Boots from the United States

A handbag from Italy

Coffee beans from Colombia

A shirt from Guatemala

Nesting dolls from Russia

A flat, 2-D map of a shopping centre

Map Key

◎	Music shop
👔	Men's clothes shop
👗	Women's clothes shop
💻	Computer shop
📚	Book shop
💍	Jewellery shop
👔👗	Department store
🧸	Toy shop
🎴	Greetings cards shop
🪑	Furniture shop
☕	Coffee shop
🎾	Sporting goods shop
👠	Shoe shop
▬	Seating area
▬	Lift
▱	Shopping centre map
▦	Escalator
⌐	Pedestrian walkway
🌸	Plants

This map shows you all the shops on the first floor of the centre. It uses **symbols** that stand for each type of shop. The map has a key. This **map key** is also called a legend. It shows you what each symbol stands for.

Find the toy shop.

Find the shoe shops.

A map of our country's resources

The United Kingdom grows many food crops. Some animals are raised to provide food and clothing. Many **natural resources** are also found here. These include coal and oil. Many man-made **goods** are also made here.

The different symbols show you where each item is found in the United Kingdom.

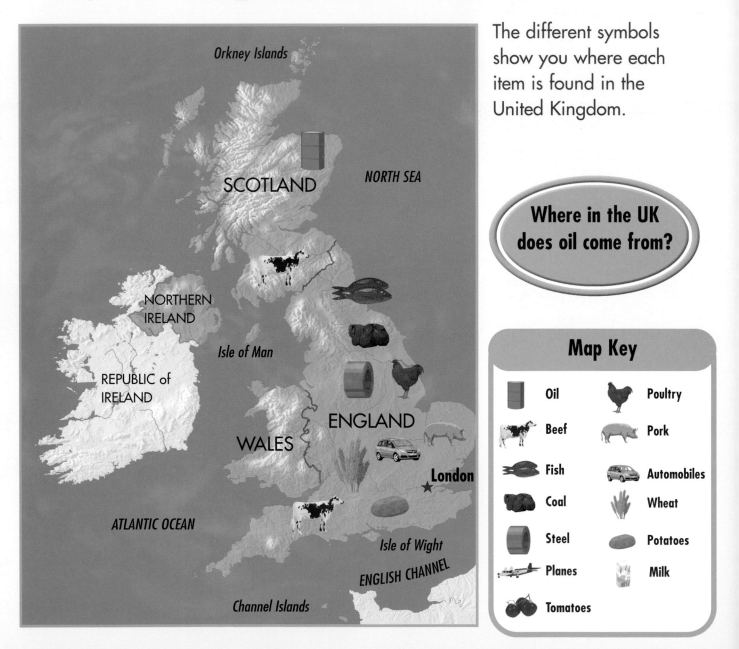

Orkney Islands

SCOTLAND

NORTH SEA

NORTHERN IRELAND

Isle of Man

REPUBLIC of IRELAND

ENGLAND

WALES

London

ATLANTIC OCEAN

Isle of Wight

ENGLISH CHANNEL

Channel Islands

Where in the UK does oil come from?

Map Key

Oil		Poultry	
Beef		Pork	
Fish		Automobiles	
Coal		Wheat	
Steel		Potatoes	
Planes		Milk	
Tomatoes			

In the United Kingdom, fish provide both an important source of food and a hobby. And when combined with another resource – potatoes – they make for a tasty treat!

What is scale?

Portsmouth

Spithead

■ Bournemouth

The Solent

ISLE of WIGHT

The Needles

ENGLISH CHANNEL

A map cannot be as big as the area it shows. In order to fit all of the real area onto a map, it must be drawn much smaller than it is in real life. This is called 'drawing to scale'.

You can more easily see cities, rivers, and other **land features** on this map of the Isle of Wight. You can also see more of its goods and natural resources.

What type of vehicles are built on the Isle of Wight?

What types of food are produced on this island?

Mapping our world

The United Kingdom is part of Europe. Europe is a very large land area called a continent. Maps of the world have seven continents on them: Europe, North America, South America, Africa, Asia, Australia, and Antarctica. Earth also has many large bodies of water. These are called oceans and seas.

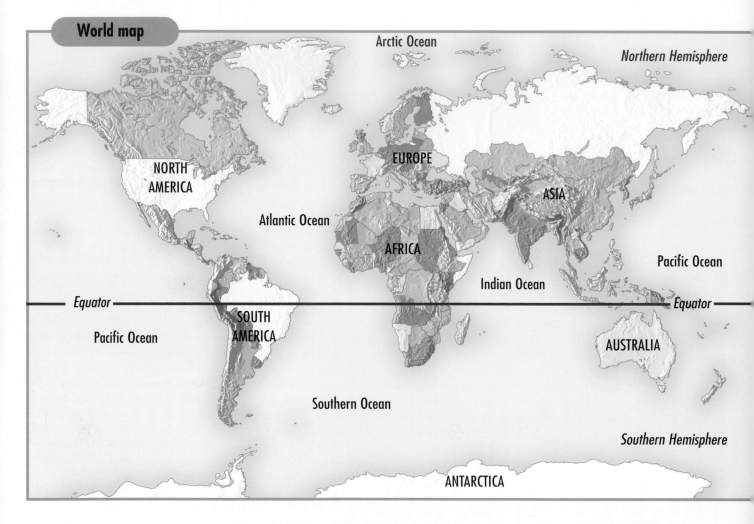

World map

Arctic Ocean

Northern Hemisphere

NORTH AMERICA

EUROPE

ASIA

Atlantic Ocean

AFRICA

Pacific Ocean

Indian Ocean

Equator

SOUTH AMERICA

Pacific Ocean

AUSTRALIA

Southern Ocean

Southern Hemisphere

ANTARCTICA

Equator

The Equator is an imaginary line. It divides Earth into two halves. One half is the Northern Hemisphere. The other half is the Southern Hemisphere. Europe is north of the Equator.

Across the Continents – a world of goods

Continents are divided into different countries. When a country sells its goods to another country, it is called **exporting**. When a country buys goods from another country, it is called **importing**. Many countries export their goods to the United Kingdom.

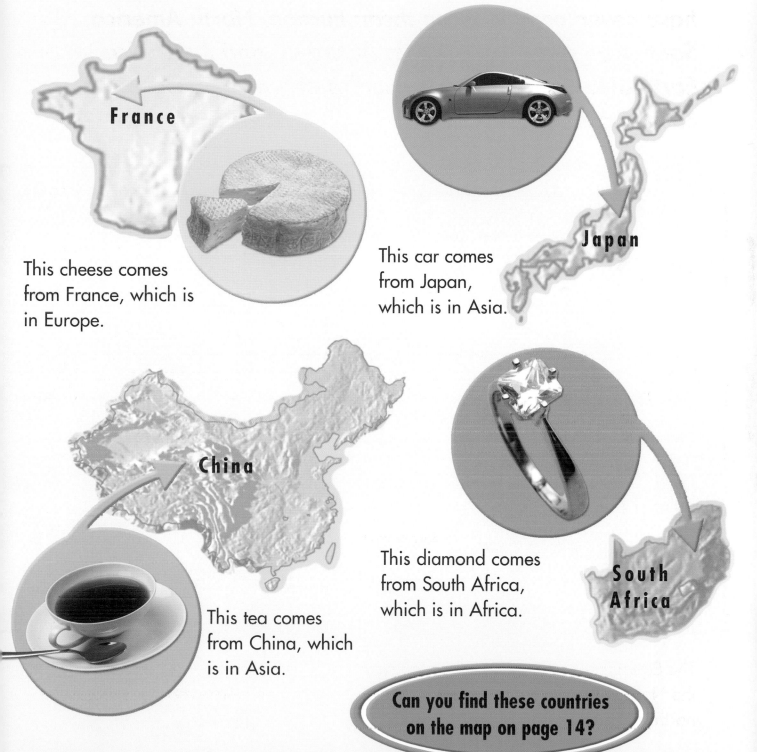

France

This cheese comes from France, which is in Europe.

Japan

This car comes from Japan, which is in Asia.

China

This tea comes from China, which is in Asia.

This diamond comes from South Africa, which is in Africa.

South Africa

Can you find these countries on the map on page 14?

A world trade map

The United Kingdom sells, or exports, many goods to other countries. It also buys, or imports, goods from other countries. This type of buying and selling is called 'trading'.

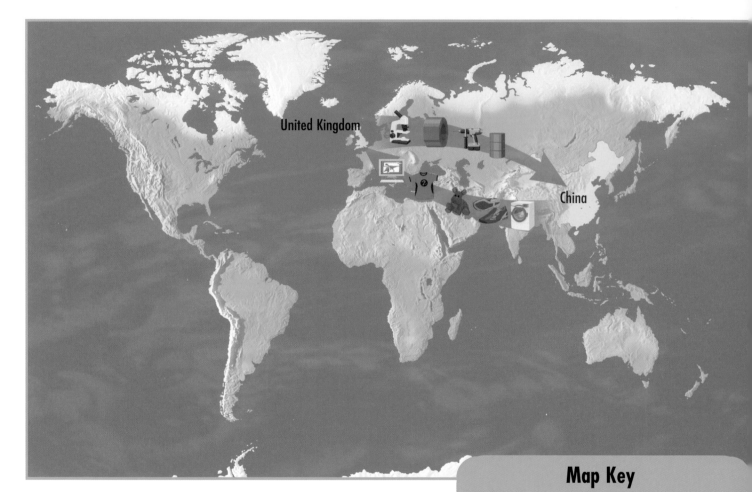

United Kingdom

China

This world map shows the kinds of things that the United Kingdom and China trade with one another.

Name a product that the UK imports from China.

Map Key

	Science instruments		Hi-tech goods
	Steel		Clothing
	Tools		Toys
	Chemicals and medicines		Shoes
			Kitchen goods

Large cargo ships are called **freighters**. They carry goods between the United Kingdom and other countries.

Cars imported from other countries are unloaded from ships at ports in the United Kingdom. The cars will be bought and used by people in the UK.

The Silk Road

Hundreds of years ago, people from different continents traded goods with one another. One of the oldest **trade routes** was called the Silk Road. It connected Asia with parts of Europe.

Silk fabrics from China.

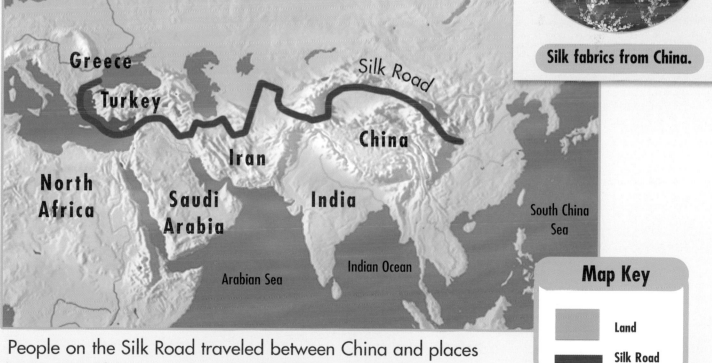

People on the Silk Road traveled between China and places in Europe. They carried pretty silk fabrics, gold, and spices.

Greece

Turkey

Silk Road

China

Iran

North Africa

Saudi Arabia

India

South China Sea

Indian Ocean

Arabian Sea

Map Key

Land

Silk Road

Mapping goods from China

China is the largest country on the continent of Asia. There are three seas along China's eastern and southern _coastline_: the Yellow Sea, East China Sea, and South China Sea.

China is a big country. Its climate and land features are different all around the country. Because China has so many different kinds of land, it grows all kinds of crops. China also has many natural resources and products.

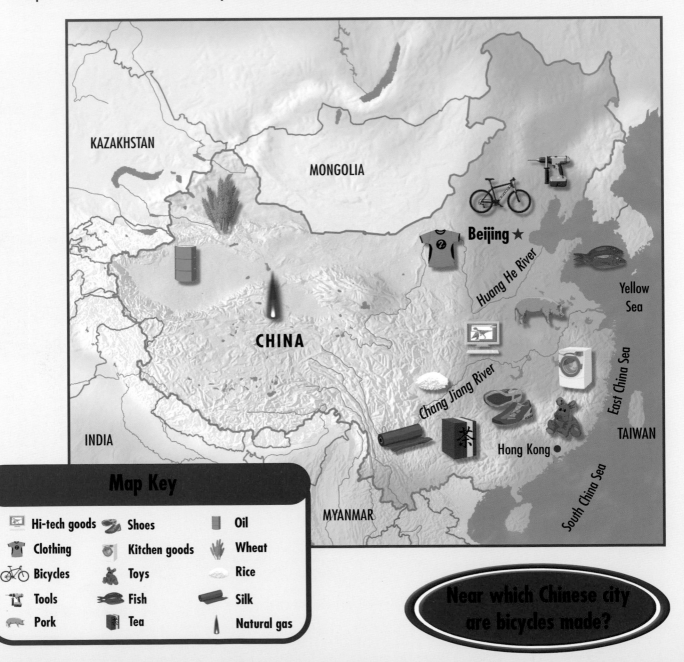

KAZAKHSTAN

MONGOLIA

Beijing ★

Huang He River

Yellow Sea

CHINA

Chang Jiang River

East China Sea

INDIA

茶

TAIWAN

Hong Kong ●

MYANMAR

South China Sea

Map Key

🖥 Hi-tech goods	👟 Shoes	▮ Oil
👕 Clothing	🍳 Kitchen goods	🌾 Wheat
🚲 Bicycles	🧸 Toys	Rice
🔧 Tools	🐟 Fish	Silk
🐖 Pork	📕 Tea	Natural gas

Near which Chinese city are bicycles made?

The mountains in China (left) are rich in minerals, such as gold, iron and coal. These minerals can be used to make products such as jewellery, metal goods, and fuel.

Tea fields grow on the warm and rainy hillsides. Rice grows in paddies where there is lots of water (right). Wheat is grown in the central and eastern plains of China. In the central and eastern farmlands, fine thread from the silk worm is gathered.

Where does silk come from?

Silkworms are caterpillars that weave their cocoons out of a single silk thread. This thread is used to make silk fabrics.

Mapping a tea farm in China

China exports tea to other countries. The tea is grown on large farms, called plantations. Many people work on tea farms in China.

Tea is planted on hillsides. Workers walk along dirt roads to get to the fields. Tall trees help protect the tea bushes from strong winds. On the edge of the field is a tea factory. The picked tea leaves are taken there to be prepared for market.

This worker hand picks the tea leaves and puts them in large baskets.

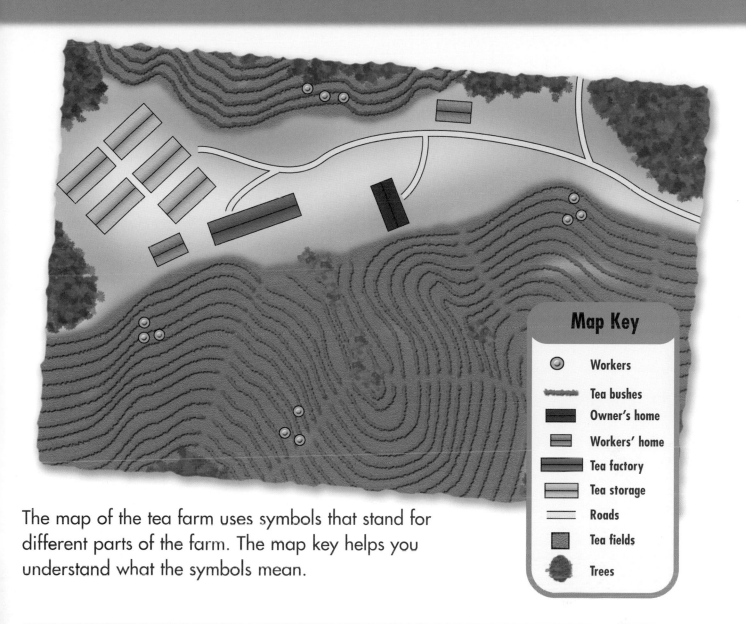

Map Key

- ⊙ Workers
- ～ Tea bushes
- ▬ Owner's home
- ▭ Workers' home
- ▬ Tea factory
- ▭ Tea storage
- ═ Roads
- ▭ Tea fields
- 🌳 Trees

The map of the tea farm uses symbols that stand for different parts of the farm. The map key helps you understand what the symbols mean.

Export and Import

China exports thousands of tons of tea to the United Kingdom. But what does it import from this country?

China imports medicines made in the United Kingdom.

Drawing maps

Before you can draw a map, you must figure out the exact size and shape of the mapping area. This means figuring out how to measure large areas.

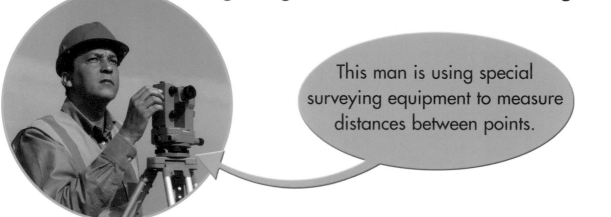

This man is using special surveying equipment to measure distances between points.

Mapmakers use their measurements to draw their maps. The maps on these pages show the attractions at an amusement park.

Scale: shrinking to fit

When mapmakers have gathered all their measurements, they must figure out how to fit them onto a piece of paper. So they shrink, or scale down, the real measurements to make a map.

0   15 metres

This small-scaled map shows a fairly large area. Many objects are visible, but they are quite small.

Different scales used to map the same area change what you see. Small-scale maps show large areas on a sheet of paper. Large-scale maps show smaller areas, but the objects look bigger and have more detail.

The map **scale** tells you how long a metre is on the map. This way you can figure out real distances on the map.

0   8 metres

This larger-scaled map shows a smaller area than the first map. The map scale also shows that each centimetre is equal to fewer metres. So you see fewer objects on this map, but you can see them in greater detail.

0   5 metres

This map has the largest scale. It shows an even smaller area. You see even fewer objects, but you can see them in even greater detail.

Hi-tech mapmaking

Many years ago, people used their travels to figure out the shape of the land. Today, mapmakers use new, hi-tech equipment.

Mapmakers can take many photographs of the ground from a plane.

This photograph shows the ground below as seen from the plane.

The pictures and measurements taken from the plane are sent to computers that draw a map.

Mapmakers also use satellites to take pictures of Earth from space.

A satellite orbiting Earth.

The pictures taken by these satellites are beamed back to Earth. They are put together to make pictures of our planet, like the one shown here. These pictures can then be turned into maps.

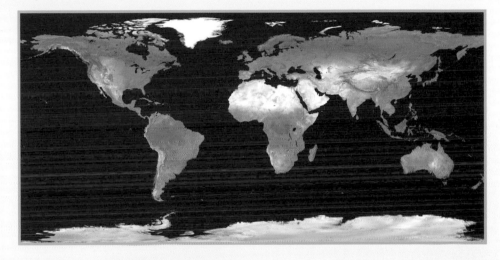

Ever-changing maps

Satellites can tell where your car is on the road. They can produce road maps that help you find your destination. These maps constantly change as you need them. The maps are called GPS, or Global Positioning System, maps.

A GPS map at work in a car.

Choosing goods to import

Pretend that you want to import goods from China. You must travel there to see them. You also want to see which of them are closest to China's largest cities. Here's how you can create a map that shows where to find the goods you want to import!

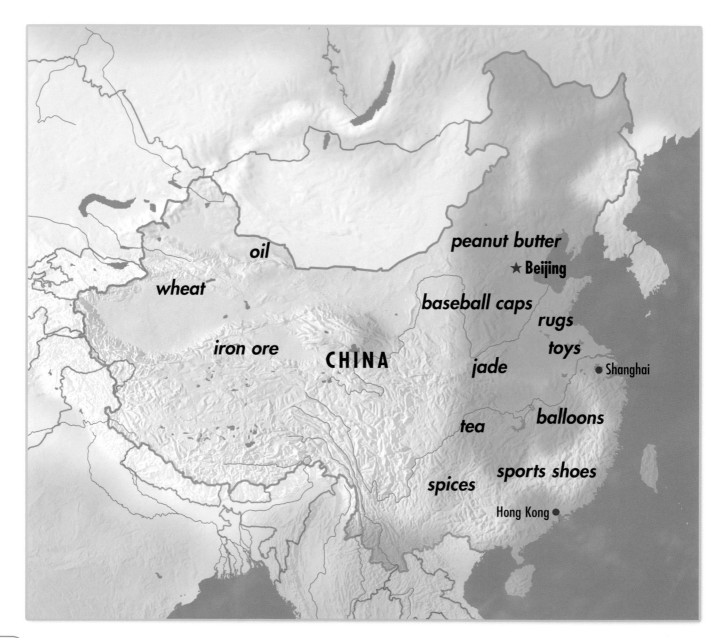

How to make a map of goods in China

1   Copy the map of China on page 26 onto a blank sheet of paper. You can also use a thin piece of tracing paper to trace the map.

2   Now make a map key. Choose some products from the list below. Draw pictures of these products in your map key.

Map Key

balloons	toys	sports shoes	wheat
oil	spices	peanut butter	rugs
jade	iron ore	tea	baseball caps

3   The map on page 26 shows where these products are made in China. Use this map as a guide to draw product pictures on your map of China. Be sure to draw the products so they look like the ones in your map key.

4   Which products are located closest to Beijing, Shanghai, and Hong Kong?

Making your own shopping centre map

Now you can design your dream shopping centre with all your favourite shops. Make a map key so your friends can see all the great things in your shopping centre.

What shape is your building? Round, square, rectangular, oval, star-shaped?

What can you buy in the shops at your shopping centre? Is there a toy shop, a book shop, or a sweet shop?

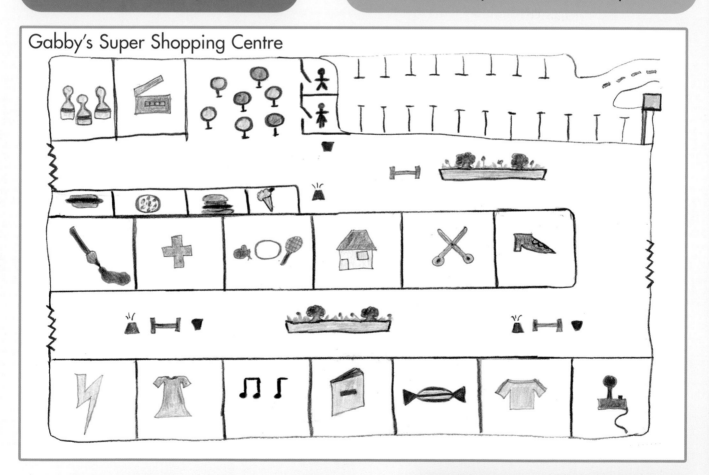

Gabby's Super Shopping Centre

What kinds of food does your shopping centre sell? Is there an ice cream shop, a doughnut shop or a pizza restaurant?

Will your centre have public toilets, indoor plants, fountains, rubbish bins or an eating area?

Step 1

Draw the shape of your shopping centre on a piece of paper. Be sure to show where the entrance is.

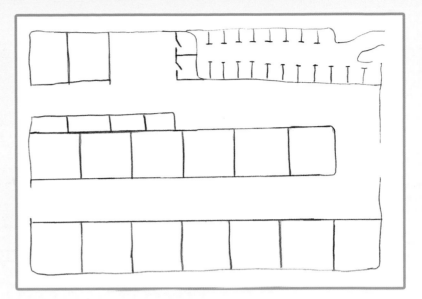

Step 2

Make up different symbols for all of the shops and other items you want to include on your map. Be sure you leave enough space between the different symbols.

Step 3

Colour your shopping centre map and give it a name!

Step 4

Make your map key using the symbols on your map.

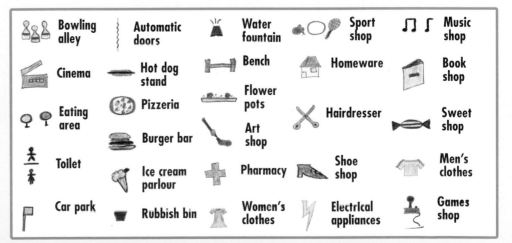

Bowling alley	Automatic doors	Water fountain	Sport shop	Music shop
Cinema	Hot dog stand	Bench	Homeware	Book shop
Eating area	Pizzeria	Flower pots	Hairdresser	Sweet shop
Toilet	Burger bar	Art shop		
	Ice cream parlour	Pharmacy	Shoe shop	Men's clothes
Car park	Rubbish bin	Women's clothes	Electrical appliances	Games shop

Glossary

Coastline: the line that forms a border between land and a body of water.

Depth: the length from top of a space or an object to its bottom.

Destination: the chosen end point of a trip.

Exporting: selling goods to another country.

Freighters: large ships used to move goods from one country to another.

Goods: items that can be sold.

GPS (Global Positioning System): an instrument that tells a driver how to get to a place. As the car is moving, the instrument shows the driver directions on a screen.

Hi-tech (high-technology) equipment: computers and other electronic products made with the most modern designs and materials.

Importing: buying goods from another country.

Land features: natural areas found on the Earth. Some are mountains, rivers, forests and deserts.

Map key: the space on a map that shows the meaning of any pictures or colours on the map.

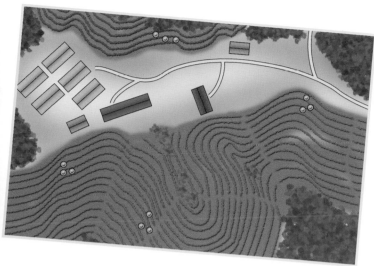

Market: a place where things are sold.

Natural resources: materials that come from the Earth and are used by people. Coal, oil, water, fish, and trees are some natural resources.

Products: items made for selling.

Satellites: objects launched into space by a rocket that circle and study Earth or other bodies in space. They then send information back to Earth.

Surveying: using special tools to measure the area of land being mapped.

Symbols: pictures or drawings that stand for different things on a map.

Three-dimensional (3-D): appearing as a solid thing that has length, width and depth.

Trade routes: travel paths used to carry goods between countries.

Two-dimensional (2-D): appearing as a flat shape with only length and width.

Index

A
Africa 14, 15
Amusement parks 22-23
Asia 14, 15

B
Beijing 26, 27

C
Cars 15, 17
China 15, 16, 17, 18-19,
  20-21, 26-27
Coastline 18, 30
Continents 14-15, 17

D
Drawing maps 22-23

E
Equator 14
Europe 14, 15, 17
Exporting 15, 16-17,
  21, 30

F
Fish 12, 13, 18
France 15
Freighters 17, 30

G
Global Positioning System
  25, 30
Goods 12, 13, 15, 16,
  17, 18, 19, 26-27, 30

H
Hi-tech mapmaking
  24-25, 30
Hong Kong 26, 27

I
Importing 15, 16-17,
  21, 30
Isle of Wight 13

J
Japan 15

M
Map key 11, 12, 21,
  27, 29, 30
Mapmaking 8-9, 10-11,
  22-23, 24-25, 26-27,
  28-29
Medicine 16, 21
Minerals 19

N
Natural resources 12-13,
  18-19, 31
North America 14
Northern Hemisphere 14

P
Paddies 19
Planes 24
Plantations 20-21
Products 10, 16, 18-19,
  27, 31

R
Rice 19
Road maps 25

S
Satellites 25, 31
Scale 13, 22-23
Seas 14
Shopping centres 10-11,
  28-29
Silk 17, 19
Silk Road 17
South Africa 15
Southern Hemisphere 14
Spices 17
Surveying 22, 31
Sweet shops 4, 8-9

T
Tea 15, 19, 20-21
Trade maps 16-17
Trade routes 17, 26-27, 31

U
United Kingdom 6, 12-13,
  14, 15, 16-17, 21

W
Weather maps 6
Wheat 19
World map 7, 14, 16